ARTICLES OF FAITH

AND

COVENANT

OF THE

FIRST PRESBYTERIAN CHURCH,

OF THE

CITY OF DETROIT.

REVISED AND PRINTED, FEBRUARY, 1850.

DETROIT:
PRINTED BY W. W. HART, BOOK & JOB PRINTER.
1850.

THE HISTORY OF THE ORIGIN, &C., OF THE FIRST PRESBYTERIAN CHURCH OF DETROIT.

The First Presbyterian Church of Detroit grew up with the first emigration of Protestant population of sufficient numbers to institute a church. From the first settlement of the place, the inhabitants were chiefly French, and belonged to the Roman Catholic faith. In 1816, on the 6th of June, the Rev. Mr. John Montieth, as a missionary commissioned by the Board of Missions of the General Assembly, of the Presbyterian Church of the United States, commenced his labors in this place. On the 5th of August, of the same year, a meeting of citizens of the Protestant faith was held, for the purpose of organizing a society for the support of religious worship. In the following May, 1817, a petition was presented to the Governor and Judges of the Territory, for a lot to be granted for a Protestant Church. In 1819, in compliance with that petition the lot now in their possession, was voted to "The First Protestant Society," which was the tittle taken by the church and congregation. The labors of Mr. Monteith had been blessed, and, during the previous year he had organized a Presbyterian Church, and ordained as Ruling Elders, Mr. J. Demming, Mr. Levi Brown, and Mr. Lemuel Shattock. He continued his labors with the congregation until January 17, 1819, when he was appointed to go abroad and solicit funds for the erection of a place of worship. On June 17, 1819, he had returned and reported that he had collected for that purpose, the sum of $1,122,46. In 1821, Mr. Montieth ceased his labors, after the first edifice had been erected where the Presbyterian lecture room now stands, on the lot granted by the Governor and Judges; and on July 23rd, of that year, when about to leave, an address was voted to him by the congregation. On the fifteenth of October, of the same year, measures were adopted to reorganize the society, which had not yet been incorporated, and, on the 30th of November afterwards a new constitution was adopted and the Trustees directed to procure an act of incorporation. On December 7th, of the same year, a call was given by the congregation to the Rev. Mr. Barrow, a Presbyterian minister in New York. Failing in this call, on the 10th of May, 1822, the trustees were authorized to employ the Rev. Mr. Welton as a supply, for such time as the pulpit might be vacant, or another person employed. In July 9, 1822, the Rev. Mr. Grattan, who had been employed, was paid for one months services as a supply. In July 11th, 1822, the Rev. Mr. Moore, who after Mr. Montieth, had been appointed and employed by the Board of Missions of the General Assembly of the Presbyterian Church as a missionary, arrived and began to labor with the congregation; and on September 22, 1822, he was employed by the congregation as a stated supply for one year. He continued to labor in the congregation until July 1, 1824, when he ceased his connection with them. In March 4, 1823. Mr. B. F. H. Witherel was appointed to procure an act of incorporation, and on the 31st of the same month, the trustees were authorized to employ a successor to Mr. Moore. In August 2nd, 1824, the Rev. Mr. Cadle was authorized to occupy the pulpit until other measures be adopted, should Mr. Moore in the mean time decline to do so. Mr. Moore did not return, and the Rev. Noah M. Wells was called, and commenced his labors as pastor in May, 1825. The Elders who had been elected and ordained in 1818, and many of the members of the church also having removed, and the church being in need of officers, it was reorganized Jan. 23, 1826, when it was found to number seven male and thirty-one female members, and Messrs, Stephen C. Henry, Eurotus P. Hastings, John J. Demming, and Asbel S. Wells were elected and ordained Ruling Elders. On February 3rd, 1827, Dr. Justin Rice, and Mr. Chas. C. Sears were ordained and added to the elderships. In August 4th, 1833, Benjamin F. Larned, Edward Bingham and H. Hallock were also ordained and added to the Eldership. Mr. Wells having resigned his pastorial relation to the church, in July, 1834, the Rev, John P. Cleveland became the pastor; and in October 8th, of the same year, Mr. Stephen Wells was ordained an Elder, and added to the session. On November 12th 1835, Mr. Robert Stuart and Chas G. Hammond were added to the Eldership; and on July 7th, 1838, Messrs. Jonathan Kearsley and David French were farther added to the session.

The Rev. Mr. J. P. Cleveland having resigned his pastoral relation to the church the Rev. Geo. Duffield, of the city of New York, having been invited to become the pastor, arrived and began to labor on the 1st of October, 1838. The call, which was unanimously addressed to him by the church and society on the of the same month, was accepted by him, and he was installed on the 11th of December following, by the Presbytery of Detroit. On the 22nd of May, 1848, Messrs. Thomas Rowland, Alexander McFarran, Alanson Sheely and Thomas J. Hulbert, were ordained and added to the Eldership, and David French was ordained as Deacon in addition to E. P. Hastings, who had been ordained such seven years before.

STATEMENT OF GENERAL PRINCIPLES.

The Session of the First Presbyterian Church of Detroit, in publishing new edition of the leading articles of its Faith and Covenant, take occasion to unfold the views and principles by which they are regulated, with respect to the admission of members into fellowship, and to the nature of the covenant binding all in union.

The Book of Discipline and Form of Government of the Presbyterian Church, which set forth the principles and order of Presbyterian government, recognize and affirm, that the duty and responsibility of judging as to the qualifications and admission of members into fellowship and of return, are devolved on the Elders together with the Pastor, who constitute the Session. (See Form of Gov. ch. 8, sec. 2., and ch. 9, sec. 6.) They have no power to make laws binding on the conscience, being merely possessed of declarative, executive and judicial authority, in the exercise of which functions regard must be had to the Law of Jesus Christ, the great and only Head of the Church. (See Prel. Prin. of the Form of Gov. ch. 1, sec. 2–7, ch. 8, sec. 2.) The word of God or Sacred

Scriptures, contain the laws by which He is pleased to govern His body; and therefore nothing ought to be, or can lawfully be, made a term of fellowship, and required in order to admission to the church, but what He has enacted; neither can any thing lawfully be omitted or compromitted, which He has ordained. (Form of Gov. ch. 1, sec. 7.) To prescribe terms of communion which Jesus Christ has not dictated, and to refuse fellowship to such as do not conform to them, is to trespass on personal liberty, to usurp His prerogative, and to make those who do so, "lords over God's heritage," in direct contravention of His own solemn interdiction. To give way and admit to fellowship, where there is not conformity, at least in the judgment of charity, an honest profession, and a promise of conformity to the commands of Jesus Christ, in any respect whatever, is to betray the trust reposed in the office-bearers of the church by its great Head, to violate their obligations to Him, and to open the door for traitors and enemies, to the great detriment of true religion, and injury of His cause and body. Such responsibilities require great seriousness, watchfulness, conscientiousness, and intelligent care and prayerfulness. Hence conversation with applicants, to enable them to examine themselves, and tender faithful attempts to ascertain their views and feelings, their experience and principles, that they may thus better judge whether they possess the qualifications which Jesus Christ has prescribed, become altogether indispensible. In judging of these things, they are to be guided by the word of God or sacred Scriptures, and to extend the privileges of His house only to those, who, in the judgment of charity, give credible evidence of their being in covenant with Him.

The Church of God, in its external visible relation to Him, as an organized body, originated with the Abrahamic covenant. (Gen. xvii, 1–13.) The Sinaitic covenant was adapted to the political relation of the Jewish people to God, as their national Sovereign and Ruler. Its ratification by no means affected the integrity or terms of the Abrahamic covenant; neither did its abrogation. (Gal. iii, 17.) The Church of God has remained *one*, organized on the *same* basis, and recognising the same terms and relation, whether under the Old or New Testament dispensation. (Eph. ii, 12–22.) The terms of the Abrahamic covenant are given in God's offer of himself as the all-sufficient One, first, on His part, to be "our shield and our exceeding great reward," and next our consent to the obligation of His command, and our sincere and honest purpose to "walk before (Him) and be perfect," involving His gracious tender of himself in like character and relation to our offspring, according to the instituted sign of His covenant, and our recognized obligations to regard them as His, and train them up for Him. Our cordial acceptance, therefore, of God as He offers himself in Christ, in the fulness and adaptation of His sufficiency to all our weekness and wants, guilt and wretchedness, for time and eternity, and the sincere consent and honest engagement of our hearts with Him to keep all His commandments, are the gracious terms of the church covenant, which God has instituted. We have no right to dictate any other. Refusing to accept Him as He offers himself to us, and to consent cordially to these obligations, no adult has any right to claim church or covenant relationship to Himself. What these terms were, or dictated to Abraham, they remain still, the covenant never having been abrogated. What are commonly called church covenants and in common use in churches, are of no value or anthority, if they are founded on any other basis. They do not, and cannot of right, originate with the church officers or society of its members, who may agree, or choose to dictate, what they will consent to in this or the other respect, and whom they will recognise or not, according to tests of their own devising, as worthy of admission. Unless the terms are what God prescribes, their covenants are of human origin, and of no authority. God alone is Lord of the conscience, and has the exclusive right to say on what terms He will receive any of us into covenant with Himself. Having done this in the Old Testament Scriptures, with the fuller exposition of the New, they must be our warrant and guide, as well, in our collective character, as churches, as in our personal character as individuals. He that does not cordially consent to the terms of God's covenant, and engage intelligently and cordially to keep all His commandments, cannot and ought not to be recognized as being in covenant with God, nor admitted to the fellowship of His church. It is at the peril of God's displeasure, and to the great injury of the church and cause of Jesus Christ, and to the peace, purity and brotherly affection of its members, that the officers of the church admit any other than those who give credible evidence of these two facts, viz. that they do intelligently, with all the heart, accept and avouch God as their God, according to the offer He makes of Himself, through Jesus Christ, and as honestly and sincerely own their obligations, and engage to keep all His commandments.

The phraseology of the formula according to which this covenant engagement with God is made, as given in this edition, is substantially in all respects the same with that heretofore in use in this church, and is also the same in substance with that which God dictated to Abraham, though expressed in language more extended and specific, and adapted to the clearer revelations of the New Testament. That part of it which specifically relates to the covenant with the church and its members, as a whole, is but the recognition of, and assent to, admitted obligations, both on the part of the members received, and of the church, as to duties which God has enjoined on all His people assumed into covenant relationship with Himself.

That the views and principles on which the Session proceed, in judging of the qualifications of those applying to be received as members of Christ's body, and what they judge to be credible evidence, of Christian character, or of genuine conversion to God, on the part of those desiring to be admitted to the fellowship of the church, there has been introduced an enumeration of certain duties and obligations which the officers of their church and its members from the beginning believe to be required and imposed directly or indirectly, in the word of God, on all who would be accounted in very deed the covenant people of God. The specification is by no means carried out in the full detail in which it is found in the word of God, but it is given merely, in some, respects as *the testimony in relation to the duties of holiness to be discharged, and the sins to be avoided, by all true christians who, to be such, must cordially recognize the authority of Jesus Christ,* and the obligations He imposes on all his covenant people and followers, without exception, to keep all the commandments of God. This testimony is given, that all may understand both the principles, and rules of God's word according to which, an estimate of christian character and of credible profession, is made in this church on the part of its officers and admitted members, and also the duties and obligations of holiness, to which, all who cordially enter into covenant with God, are required sincerely to consent to, conscientiously to aim to discharge, before God, and unblameably to observe before men. They are also part and parcel of that testimony, which as witnesses for Jesus Christ, all his professed followers are bound, in their lives and conversation, to bear, according to His word, for the reproof and benefit of a world which lieth in wickedness, as well as for His glory. With his deficiencies in heart *before God* in any respect, each one has to do with Him alone, in the way of private confession to Him, and repentance before Him. As to instances of failure, in the sight of man, through prevalent temptation on the part of any who profess religion, while the obligation binds to warn, reprove, rebuke, exhort, and entreat, as the circumstances of the case may require, the sacred Scriptures impose on the officers of the church, solemn responsibilities, duly to weigh all those circumstances, and to judge whether there has been such an absolute vitiation of all claims to christian character, as to call for their ejection from the fellowship of the church, and how far forbearance and forgiveness may be rendered necessary to reclaim the erring and bring the backsliding to repentance. Occasional acts, determined by the force of temptation, hold a very different place in the estimate of christian character, from those which are wilful, deliberate, repeated, persisted in and habitual, proving the settled bias of the will or inclination and purpose of the heart.

There have been added also, as helps for holy living and self-examination, various resolutions and questions which are recommended to the occasional perusal of the members of the church, and which it is hoped may be blessed of God to their advancement and stability in the divine life.

In conclusion, the officers of the church desire and solicit the constant prayers and the cordial, conscientious and brotherly co-operation of all the members of the church over whom they are called to watch as those who must give an account, so that God's blessing may ever rest upon us as His covenant people, and He be graciously pleased to own and employ us, as instruments in His hand, not only for our mutual edification, but for the conviction and conversion, and bringing into His covenant, of them that are without.

FORM OF INTRODUCTION INTO THE FIRST PRESBYTERIAN CHURCH OF DETROIT, MICH.

(The pastor shall address the persons, whom the Session have admitted, when, upon their names being called, they shall have appeared before the church, immediately prior to the administratlon of the Lord's Supper; and he shall make the following or similar remarks:)

ADDRESS.

BELOVED IN THE LORD: You, who for the first time approach this table of the Lord, have here presented yourselves, before God and this church, to profess your faith in Jesus Christ, and your covenant engagements to serve Him, and also publicly to incorporate yourselves with these its members in full and visible membership. Your present act does not constitute you members, having already been admitted as such by the vote of the Session. It merely introduces you to your brethren and sisters in Christ, with whom you engage to walk according to the faith and order of the gospel as professed by this church. Neither does your present act create any obligations to serve God, that did not previously exist; but merely recognizes, and renews your assent to, those which you now see you ought to have discharged, ever since you were capable of understanding the divine claims upon your conscience. It is your sin that you have so long refused to own them. And you now confess your past rebellion, and declare your hearty surrender of yourselves to God, the Father, the Son, and the Holy Spirit, in all the offices they discharge for the government and salvation of men, as well as your deliberate purpose to live in subjection to Christ, and to identify your interests, for ever with Him and His church.

We trust that this thing has been seriously and carefully considered by you. It is solemn in its nature; and its consequences will be eternal. God, angels and men, are witnesses of this transaction. It will be recorded in Heaven and on earth, and will live in your own delightful or mournful remembrance, amid the songs of the redeemed or the wailings of the lost.

Yet with these reflections you need not be overwhelmed. You come at the command of Jesus Christ to confess Him before men as your divine Lord and Master, who has said, "My grace is sufficient for thee, for my strength is made perfect in weakness." Gal. 12: 9.

You, too, beloved, who have been received into the fellowship of this church, upon your letters of dismission and recommendation from sister churches, do also here present yourselves, to own your obligations, and to covenant to walk in fellowship with this church according to the faith and order of the gospel here professed. We cordially greet you, and welcome you to this fold of Jesus Christ, hoping and praying, that your fellowship with us, may be as profitable and pleasurable to you, as that from which, in the providence of God, you have been removed. Attend to the

CONFESSION OF FAITH.

I.

There is ONE GOD, Father, Son, and Holy Gost, who created all things by the word of His power, for His own glory.

Dut. vi. 4; 1 Cor. viii. 6; 1 John. v. 7; 2 Cor. xiii. 14; Col. i. 16.

II.

God is eternal in his existence, immutable in his purposes, universal in his providence, infinite in power, wisdom, justice, goodness, and truth.

1 Tim. i, 17 ; 3 Psh. i, 9–11 ; Luk. xii, 5–7 ; Jude. v, 25–2.

III.

God is the only proper object of religious worship, and is worthy of supreme love, and constant obedience.

1 Thes. i, 10 ; Exod. xx, 3–5 ; Math. xxii, 37 ; John. xv, 10.

IV.

JESUS CHRIST is God and man, having two distinct natures and one person.

Phil. ii, 5–11 ; Heb. i, 3–8–10 ; ii, 14; Col. i, 15–19.

V.

The Scriptures of the Old and New Testament were given by inspiration of God, and are a perfect rule of faith and practice.

2 Tim. iii, 16–17 ; 1 Pet. i, 10–12 ; 2 Pet. i, 16–20.

VI.

Man was originally created in a state of innocence, but by voluntary transgression, became a sinner, and all his posterity are naturally destitute of holiness, and, therefore, under condemnation by the law of God.

Gen. i, 26 ; Eccl. vii, 29 ; Rom. v, 12 ; viii, 5–8.

VII.

Jesus Christ, as the only Mediator between God and man, has made an atonement for the sins of the world, so that God is just in justifying all who believe upon His name.

1 Tim. ii, 5–6 ; 1 John. ii, 1–2 ; Rom. iii, 25–26.

VIII.

The justification of a sinner before God, is an act of His grace, by which He accepts him as righteous, not for any worthiness of his own, but wholly on account of the righteousness of Jesus Christ received by faith.

Rom. viii, 1–4 ; iii, 28 ; iv, 5–8.

IX.

Justifying faith is not mere knowledge or assent, but a believing with the heart ; and its virtue to save, is not because of its being a deed of righteousness, the substance of holiness, or the sum of obedience ; but as it is the means of union with Christ, of adoption into His family, and of receiving the benefits of His redemption.

Rom. x, 3–10 ; Tit. iii, 4–7 ; Gal. ii, 16–21 ; John. i, 12.

X.

Love to God, repentance for sin, and a life of holiness, are the certain consequences and the indispensable evidence of justification by faith.

Rom. vi, 1–33.

XI.

Nothing prevents repentance and salvation but voluntary continuance in sin, yet none will ever repent, or be saved, *without the influence of the* HOLY SPIRIT.

Jer. vii, 23–28 ; 1 Cor. xii, 3.

XII.

God has determined to secure the salvation of some, and all such will be renewed by his Spirit, kept by his power, and saved by his grace.

Eph. i, 4, 5 ; 1 Pet. i, 3–8.

XIII.

The Sacraments of the New Testament are baptism, and the Lord's Supper. The former is to be administered to such as publicly profess their faith in Christ and to their households; the latter, only to those members of christian churches, who are in good standing.

Math. xxviii, 19; 1 Cor. xi, 23–26; Acts. viii, 37; xvi, 31–33.

XIV.

There will be a resurrection of the dead; both of the righteous and the wicked.

Dan. xii, 2; John. v, 28–29.

VII.

There will be a day of general Judgment, when all mankind will receive a just sentence of retribution, according to the deeds done in the body; and the punishment of the wicked, as well as the happiness of the righteous, will be ENDLESS.

Rev. xx, 12, 13; xxi, 7, 8.

Thus you profess to believe: attend now to

THE COVENANT.

You do now, in the sight of God, confess your past opposition to Him,[1] your impenitent and unbelieving rejection of Christ,[2] and the manifold transgressions of your lives,[3] in your unconverted state; all which you cordially condemn and renounce;[4] but believing, that there is mercy freely offered to you through Jesust Christ,[5] —and that you have in His Word an ample warrant[6] to look to Him for pardon and salvation,[7] to confide in, and appropriate Him,[8] as your prophet to instruct you,[9] your priest to atone for your sins,[10] and your King and Lord to have dominion over you,[11]—you do solemnly avouch[12] God the Father, the Son, and the Holy Spirit, the One only living and true God, to be your God,[13] the object of your supreme affection, and your everlasting portion,[14]—freely accepting and choosing the Father to be your Father,[15] the Son to be your all sufficient Redeemer,[16] Intercessor, and only Mediator,[17] and the Holy Spirit to be your Teacher, Sanctifier, Comforter and Guide.[18]

[1] Isai. i, 2. [2] Isai. liii, 3. [3] Psalm xxxii, 3: li, 3. [4] Job xlii, 6. [5] Jer. iii, 12: Jude 21. [6] Psalm cxix, 58. [7] Isai. xlv, 22. [8] Psalm lxii, 8. [9] Deut. xviii, 15. [10] Heb. iv, 14—16. [11] Isai. xxvi, 13. [12] Deut. xxvi, 17, 18. [13] Psalm xlviii, 14: lxviii, 20. [14] Psalm xviii 1, 2: cxix, 57. [15] Isai. lxiii, 13: lxiv, 8. [16] Psalm xix, 14. [17] I Tim. ii, 5. [18] John xiv. 15, 16, 26.

Renouncing the world,[1] the flesh,[2] and the devil,[3] with all their ungodly and worldly lusts,[4] you do now freely, in the fixed choice and purpose of your hearts,[5] give up yourselves, soul, spirit and body, to be the Lord's[6] for ever.

[1] Jam. iv, 4: I John ii, 15. [2] Gal. v, 24. [3] II Tim. ii, 25, 26: I John iii, 8, 10. [4] Tit. ii, 12. [5] Psalm lvii, 7: Psalm lxxiii, 24—26. [6] I Thes. v, 23: Psalm xvi, 2: Josh. xxiv, 15.

You promise and covenant, to walk before Him in Holiness and Righteousness, all the days of your life,[1] sincerely endeavoring, in reliance on His grace, to perform every known duty, to forsake every known sin, especially your besetting sins,[2] to conquer every sinful passion,[3] to walk after the example of Christ,[4] to avoid all sinful stumbling blocks, and occasions of offence, as becomes the disciples of the meek and lowly Jesus, and to adorn the doctrine of God our Saviour.[5]

[1] I Thess. iii, 12, 13: II Cor. vii, 1. [2] Eph. v, 21, 22, 25: vi, 1, 4, 5, 6, 7, 9: I Pet. ii, 13, 14. [3] Gal. v, 24: I Pet. ii, 11. [4] Eph. v, 1, 2: I Pet. ii, 21. [5] Gal. v. 19–26: Tit. ii, 10–12.

You receive the members of this church as your brethren and sisters in Christ, and promise to exercise, with tenderness and fidelity, a christian watch and care over them, as far as you may have knowledge and opportunity.[1]

[1] Heb. iii, 12, 13: I Thess. v, 14.

You promise also and covenant, to submit to the government of Christ, in his church, and while you continue with us, to the regular and lawful administration of the same, in this church in particular, [1] which, to be such, must be agreeably to the Confession of Faith, the Form of Government, and Book of Discipline, which form the constitutional standards of the Presbyterian church in these United States,[2] and which we recommend to your frequent perusal; and when, in the providence of God, you may be called to reside elsewhere, to ask and take with you, letters of dismission and recommendation, with a view to enter into visible fellowship with some christian church, where the ordinances of the gospel may be maintained, and your lot may be cast.[3]

[1] Heb. xiii, 7, 17: I Tim. v, 17: I Thess. v, 12, 13. [2] Phil. iii, 16, 17–19: II Thess. iii, 6. [3] I Cor. xiv, 33.

THE TESTIMONY.—Acts I, 8 : Mat. X, 32, 33.

(Here the pastor shall address the persons covenanting, briefly, or in a more extended manner, according as he may think time or circumstances may require or suggest, and either refer to, or read at length, the following testimony as to the life of holiness which God requires, and the church expects, in all her members.)

Ordinarily, he may say to them :

In thus covenanting with God and this church, we expect you cordially and conscientiously to unite with us, by your blameless walk and conversation, in maintaining that TESTIMONY, according to the word of God, borne by this church, in favor of the duties of holiness, which all who porfess the religion of Jesus Christ, are bound to lead, and against those sins of the world that lieth in wickedness, which all are bound to forsake.

(When the above is read, the following is to be omitted ; or, on particular occasions, he may omit the foregoing, and read as follows :)

In thus covenanting with God and his church, beloved brethren and sisters in Christ, we expect you cordially and conscientiously to unite with us in bearing common TESTIMONY by a blameless walk and conversation, in favor of the duties of a life of holiness, and against the sins of the world that lieth in wickedness, Eph. i, 4, and iv, 17–19; according as the word of God sets forth those obligations, viz:

I. To observe Secret and Family Prayer. Mat. vi, 5, 6 : Josh. xxiv, 15.

II. To Sanctify the Sabbath—by abstaining from all worldly business, traveling, and recreations on that day, and by appropriating it to the purposes of divine worship. Isai. lviii, 13 : Exod. xx, 8, &c.

III. To observe the Ordinances which God has appointed :

1. By attending and contributing to maintain His worship and the preaching of His gospel, especially as established in this church. Heb. x, 25 : Luke i, 6.

2. By frequenting the Lord's Supper, especially when here administered. 1 Cor. xi, 23–26.

3. By dedicating to Him, in Baptism, when parents, the children God hath given, and by training them up to walk in obedience to His

commands, and observance of His ordinances. Gen. xvii, 7–14 : Rom. xi, 11–18: Rom. ii, 28, 29 : iv, 9–16 : Col. ii, 11, 12 : Acts ii, 38, 39 : xvi, 31, 33 : 1 Cor. i, 16.

IV. To Cultivate Christian Fellowship and Brotherly Love :

1. By studying to be more and more conformed, in spirit and behaviour, to Jesus Christ. Eph. v, 1, 2.

2. By not taking up a reproach against a brother or sister. Psalm xv, 3 : Lev. xix, 16–18.

3. By not impeaching the motives, nor condemning the character and conduct of a brother or sister on mere rumor or suspicion. Mat. vii, 1–5.

4. By refraining from all back-biting, speaking evil of, and circulating injurious accusations, against the character of a brother or sister; especially, if there is not personal knowledge of the things alleged ; or there may be an unwillingness and neglect to visit, and in private conversation, obtain, if false, denials of such injurious accusations or reports ; if misstatements, such explanations as may remove the scandal ; or if true, to do what Christ has enjoined to bring the offending to repentance, or to promote the peace, purity and welfare of the church. Psalm xv, 3 : Mat. xviii, 15–17.

5. By maintaining uprightness, honesty, and sincerity, in worldly transactions and social intercourse. Psalm xv, 2, 4 : 1 Cor. v, 8 : 2 Cor. i, 12.

6. By guarding against whatever, in conduct or conversation, is inconsistent with a christian profession, and injurious, to the spiritual welfare of christian brethren, to the reputation, influence and usefulness of the church, and to the interests of vital godliness. Psalm 101: 1–7 : 1 Thess. iv, 12 : v, 22 : Phil. iv, 8.

V. To Renounce the World which lieth in Wickedness :

1. By coming out from the fellowship of wicked and ungodly men. 2 Cor. vi, 17, 18 : Eph. v, 11 : 1 Cor. v, 9–11 : 2 Thess. iii. 6, 14, 15.

2. By refusing to co-operate with wicked and ungodly persons in their sinful works and enjoyments. Psalm cxli, 4

VI. To avoid all those Customs and Recreations which lead others to Sin:

1. Such as giving and partaking of intoxicating liquors as a beverage.* 1 Tim. v, 22: Rev. xviii, 3: Heb. ii, 15: 1 Cor. ix, 22, 27 Rom. xiv. 21: Eph. v, 7, 18: Isai. v, 12.

2. Public balls, dancing parties, theatres, and whatever places of amusement are inconsistent with, and destroy confidence in, christian character and profession, wound the cause of Christ, injure the godly reputation of the church, or prove stumbling blocks in the way of impenitent and unbelieving men. Isai. v, 12: iii, 16: Mack. v, 22: Rom. xiii, 13: Eph. ii, 2, 3: vi, 11, 15: 1 Pet. iv, 3: Rom. xiv, 13: xii, 1–3: Phil. i, 27.

(Here all the members of the church rising, the minister shall address those introduced at the time, as follows, in testimony of Acceptance:)

Beloved Brethren and Sisters in Christ: We, the members and officers of this church, being pleased and satisfied with your professions and engagements, cordially recognize you as members with us, and welcome you to our fellowship; and we promise and covenant, through divine grace, to receive and love you as christians, to exercise a brotherly watch and care over you, to pray for you and to seek your confidence as long as you shall continue with us.

(The church being seated, the minister will address the new members as follows, in some such words of Exhortation:)

Beloved in the Lord: You have witnessed a good confession; you have recognized and assented to engagements from which you can never escape. Your vows will meet you at the bar of God. You can

* Note. This testimony the church adopted specially, after the matter had been submitted by the Session for consideration, and discussed at four successive meetings of members. It was embodied in a report brought in by Messrs. E. Bingham, Geo. E. Hand and A. Sheeley, adopted by the church March 31, 1841, and pressed on the attention of all in a pastoral letter, addressed to the members in pursuance of said report, and adopted by the Session April 22, 1841, and signed by the moderator and all the elders.

Copies of the resolutions of the Church and Session will be found in the appendix.

never be as you have been, but must henceforth and forever be the servants of God. Apostacy will lead to perdition. From the holy and reasonable obligations you have just recognized, you can never absolve yourselves. Nor can you separate yourselves from God's visible church, and cease to walk with his professing people, without being guilty of covenant breaking, becoming traitors to Jesus Christ, and exposing yourselves to the righteous displeasure of God. You cannot be justified in absenting yourselves from the worship and ordinances of Christ's house, for any other reason than such as may be resolved into the directing overruling and controling providence of God. You are the Lord's by your own act of self-commitment and consecration, and we trust that you will ever hereafter sincerely desire and consistently aim to live for His glory to whom you have now consecrated yourselves. The eyes of the world will be upou you. As you demean yourselves consistently or otherwise, so will religion, and this church, through you, be honored or disgraced. If you live according to the gospel, you will be a comfort to us, but if not, a stumbling-block, a grief and a vexation. And if there be a wo pronounced upon him who offends *one* of Christ's little ones, wo! wo! wo! be to the person who offends a whole church. But, beloved, we hope better things of you, and things that accompany salvation, though we thus speak. We charge you forget not this day and these engagements. Be faithful unto death. Be holy in all manner of conversation and godliness, "looking for and hasting unto the coming of the day of God;" and may the God of all peace and consolation keep your minds and hearts in Christ Jesus, waiting for the mercy of God unto eternal life. Grace be with you all. Amen.

APPENDIX.

RESOLUTIONS AND QUESTIONS.

The following resolutions, designed to direct the members of the church in maintaining a consistent walk, are recommended to their careful observance and frequent perusal:

1. *Resolved*. That I will make it a matter of conscience to attend all the meetings for social worship appointed by the church, except when prevented by the providence of God, and endeavor not to fear or be ashamed when called on to take part in them.

2. *Resolved*, That I will make it a matter of conscience to do what I can by my pecuniary ability, to promote the cause of the Redeemer, and that I will take care punctually to discharge my pecuniary obligations to this church as they become due.

3. *Resolved*, That I will sincerely desire, and pray, and labor, for the salvation of my children, and such youth, whether apprentices or others, as may be committed to my care, making it a matter of conscience to maintain regularly the worship of God in my family.

4. *Resolved*, That I will keep my tongue from speaking evil of a brother or sister of the church, and if in any thing I become displeased with such, I will follow the gospel rule* and tell him or her my feelings between ourselves alone.

5. *Resolved*, That I will cultiva.e a spirit of christian tenderness towards the failings and imperfections of my brethren, and if at any time I think their conduct reprehensible, I will admonish them before I allow myself to speak of it to others.

6. *Resolved*, That I will make it a matter of conscience never to visit any place of amusement, or seek any place of pleasure, on which I cannot first ask the divine blessing, or where it may be deemed iutrusive to introduce the subject of religion.

7. *Resolved*, That I will hold myself ready to forgive, and will pray for my enemies.

8. *Resolved*, That I will deny myself every sinful gratification, and the indulgence of every improper passion, and endeavor to be instrumental in bringing sinners to repentance.

9. *Resolved*, That in the prosecution of my worldly business, I will rather suffer loss than be guilty of any act of injustice, oppression, deception, or fraud.

10. *Resolved*, That I will never abuse or impeach the motives of my fellow christians when they may ask me for pecuniary aid for some benevolent purpose, and that I will endeavor to act in all cases agreeably to the obligations that rest on those whom God holds responsible as his stewards.

[The following questions are affectionately recommended to the prayerful and frequent perusal of each member of this church, and are designed to aid in the discharge of the duty of self-examination :]

1. Are you in the practice of daily secret prayer ?

2. Are you in the practice of daily family prayer ?

3. Do you, daily, with a prayerful desire to improve in christian knowledge, read the word of God ? and do you feel it to be your duty to attend, whenever you can, the weekly lecture, at which the sacred scriptures are regularly expounded ?

4. Do you feel it to be your duty to do something, as opportunity offers, to bring sinners to repentance ?

5. Do you pray every day that God would bless his truth to the conviction and conversion of sinners ?

6. Are you doing any thing to further the salvation of the rising generation, in Sabbath schools and Bible classes ?

7. Are you at peace with all who love Christ ?

8. If you are at variance with a christian professor, will you go without delay, and if you have been injured, proffer forgiveness, and if you have done the injury, profess repentance and make amends for it ?

9. Are you as tender of the reputation of a brother as of your own ?

10. Do you labour to promote your own and the sanctification of your brethren ?

11. Do you pray daily for your minister and the officers of this church?

12. Do you labor to keep your heart constantly alive to a sense of obligation. 1. To God. 2. To all the friends of the Saviour. 3. To your perishing fellow creatures?

13. Do you feel it to be your duty to consecrate all you have and are, to the Lord?

14. Have you done or said any thing out of revenge or envy, and if so, will you immediately repent of it?

15. Do you maintain strict temperance in eating and drinking, abstaining from the use of intoxicating liquors as a beverage and from all appearance of evil?

16. Are you careful when you hear an ill-natured or injurious remark in reference to a christian brother, either to admonish the person who has made it or never repeat it yourself?

17. Are you careful in narations never to speak any thing as true except, what you know to be so, and do you beware of asserting as truth what is only your own inference or conjecture or suspicion.

18. Do you sanctify the Sabbath by avoiding all trifling conversation, and paying of visits on that day, and the spending more than an ordinary portion of it in sleep, by appropriating it carefully to the purposes of divine worship, and especially some portion of it more than ordinary to secret prayer and meditation?

19. Do you extend your christian charity to the members of all such religious denominations as profess Evangelical piety?

20. Will you read these questions and the preceding resolutions before each communion season at least, and pray God to search your heart in reference to the several points of christian practice suggested by them.

NOTICES.

Public worship is observed every Sabbath at stated hours, varying according to the season.

There is a weekly Lecture every Wednesday evening, and a general prayer meeting every Friday evening.

A Female Bible class is held every Thursday afternoon during the winter season, and the children catechised the same afternoon.

The first Sabbaths in January, March, May, July, September and November, are the stated periods for the commemoration of the death of Christ, in the sacrament of the Lord's Supper.

RESOLUTIONS

Adopted at a meeting of the Members of the First Presbyterian Church of Detroit, held March 31, 1841.

Whereas, intemperance prevails to a sad extent in this place, notwithstanding all the efforts heretofore made to prevent it; and whereas, christian duty, and consistency of christian conduct in the exhibition of examples of temperance and self-denial, and every virtue, impose especial obligations and responsibilities, on members of the church of Jesus Christ; and whereas, the renewed zeal of the friends of temperance, and present circumstances propitious to the reformation of the habits of society, in reference to the use of intoxicating drinks, together with the success attendant on the judicious efforts of temperance societies, call for an expression of our sentiments and action, appropriate to our character as professed friends and followers of Jesus Christ: therefore,

Resolved, That as members of the church of our Lord Jesus Christ, we approve of temperance societies formed on the principle of entire abstinence from intoxicating liquors used as a beverage, and recommend them as being calculated to prove efficient means of preventing the increase and ravages of intemperance; and we feel bound in duty to God, to his cause, to our fellow men, and to the interests of society, to abstain ourselves entirely from the traffic in, or use of, intoxicating liquors as a beverage, and to withhold the presentation of them in our families, to others, and to discourage by our example and influence, the use of them in society.

Resolved, further, That although we cannot but regret, if any of our immediate brethren, or any of the members of any other church of our Lord Jesus Christ, whatever, should not feel it to be their duty to practice entire abstinence from all intoxicating drinks, and to discourage the use of them in others, yet, nevertheless, without attempting or claiming any right to judge our brethren, we would earnestly recommend to such, the serious and prayerful consideration of this subject, and affectionately to inquire whether they should not feel themselves morally bound, if not to adopt the temperance pledge, at least, themselves, to practice on the principles of total abstinence from intoxicating liquors as a beverage, and to discourage the use of them in others.

Resolved, That the preamble and resolutions just adopted, be copied into a blank book of suitable size, and placed in the hands of the pastor; and that every member of this church be affectionately requested to subscribe his or her name to the same. That the Pastor and members of the session be requested to sign their names first.

Resolved, That the resolutions lately adopted on the subject of temperance, be transmitted to the session, with our earnest request that they will recommend such further measures, as may be the best and most efficient for the church to take in this matter.

April 15, 1841, the above resolutions were laid before session; were-upon,

The session, after having maturely considered the subject, unanimously adopted the following resolutions, and directed the clerk to spread them upon the records:

Resolved, That we deem it important for the advancement of any great enterprise, yea, essential to its ultimate and permanent success, that the members of the church of our Lord and Saviour, Jesus Christ, should be united in their views and practice, and both individually and conjointly endeavor, by the avowal of their principles, and by conformity and harmony of practice, to promote it.

Resolved, That the evils of intemperance are so great and wide spread, and desolating, that it behoves every member of the church to set his face against it, and to endeavor, to the utmost extent of his influence, to counteract it.

Resolved, That the true and only consistent example of temperance which can be set by members of the church, is to abstain entirely from the use, manufacture and sale of intoxicating liquors as a beverage, and to withhold the presentation of them to others, and that the session of this church feel bound and determined, themselves, to maintain such an example.

Resolved, That we feel it to be very desirable that all the members of this church should embody their influence, and by a uniform, consistent example of total abstinence from intoxicating liquors, bear their testimony in favor of the temperance cause, and therefore earnestly and affectionately recommend to all, both male and female, seriously and prayerfully to consider the resolutions adopted at a meeting of the church, either by the avowal of their determination, or by attaching their signatures to some temperance pledge, to express their purpose of co-operation in the important efforts now making for the prevention of intemperance.

Resolved, That while we feel bound to disapprove every thing like an attempt to institute a summary test of pity, or to appoint terms of church membership which Jesus Christ, the great Head of the church, has not appointed, and while we deprecate and condemn all rash, hasty and invidious use of the system of pledges for this purpose, we nevertheless feel bound to declare that as office bearers in Christ's church, on whom devolves the responsibility of admitting members, we cannot but deem it to be utterly inconsistent with a credible profession of true religion, for those, who having been enlightened on the subject of the immorality of the use, sale and manufacture of intoxicating liquors as a beverage, nevertheless, refuse to discontinue the same.

Resolved, That the session deem it expedient, at present, to take any action in reference to the enrolment of the members of the church, in a book, agreeably to their third resolution, but that the Pastor and Elder Bingham, be a committee, to prepare a pastoral letter from the session, to accompany the resolutions from the church and session, and cause the same to be printed, and a copy to be furnished to each member of this church.

(From the records.)

B. F. LARNED,
Clerk.

ERRATA.—Page 3, line 12, for *Protestant*, read *Presbyterian*. Insert in the blank, on page 5, "22d of October, 1838." Page 8, line 15 from the bottom, for *their*, read *this*.

www.ingramcontent.com/pod-product-compliance
Lightning Source LLC
LaVergne TN
LVHW011143110826
845150LV00008B/2485